"Beastie" Poems

Geza Tatrallyay

Cover: Vectors by Vecteezy https://www.vecteezy.com/free-vector/animals
ISBN: 978-81-19654-85-7

First Edition: 2023
Rs. 200/- $15

Cyberwit.net
HIG 45 Kaushambi Kunj, Kalindipuram
Allahabad - 211011 (U.P.) India
http://www.cyberwit.net
Tel: +(91) 9415091004
E-mail: info@cyberwit.net

Printed at Repro India Limited.

For my grandchildren

Introduction

I have been writing poems for most of my life, first starting with some efforts in my native Hungarian, then translating some of the greats from languages I was learning—Goethe, Rilke, Baudelaire among others—until, finally, trying my hand at English, which since then has become the language I am most comfortable with for all my writing. Now, later in life, I am writing more poetry, with some of it published in different journals in the USA and Canada. I am fortunate that P.R.A. Publishing published my first collection, *Cello's Tears*, in 2015, and then as well my second, *Sighs and Murmurs*, in 2017, and my third, *Extinction*, in 2019. A subsequent collection, *Extinction Rebellion*, was published in 2020 by Cyberwit, an Indian publisher of poetry, while my fifth collection *The Abyss: Poems for our World* was released in September 2022 by Deux Voiliers Publishing.

I conceived the idea for this little book several years ago when I was compiling *Extinction*, my third volume of poetry, noting that many of my poems celebrate the different species of animate life around us that we are endangering with our consumption-oriented lifestyle. These "beastie" poems are dotted throughout my five collections, so I brought the published ones and some unpublished ones together to create this volume and included a couple of poems at the beginning and the end that deride what we are doing to our fellow beings—driving them to extinction—but also cry out for a new beginning. The poems in between celebrate, or at least touch on, the many animal species I have come across in different situations. I hope the sense of wonder at each magnificent form of life and in magic of evolution comes through in my writing, as does the precarious situation that our lifestyle is creating for the world and all life on it.

I am delighted that Cyberwit has agreed to publish this, my sixth collection of poetry. I hope my readers will take as much pleasure in reading the poems as I did in the writing, and that the volume will spur some thinking of what we can do to better safeguard the living species around us.

Geza Tatrallyay
November, 2023

Geza's Other Books

Arctic Meltdown, (thriller) e-published on Amazon and www.smashwords.com, December 2011

Twisted Reasons, (thriller, first in 'Twisted' trilogy) November 2014, Deux Voiliers Publishing

Cello's Tears, (poetry collection) May 2015, P.R.A. Publishing

For the Children, (memoir) May 2015, Editions Dedicaces

The Expo Affair, (memoir) April 2016, Guernica Editions

Twisted Traffick, (thriller, second in 'Twisted' trilogy) October 2017, Black Opal Books

Sighs and Murmurs, (poetry collection) April 2018, P.R.A. Publishing

Twisted Fates, (thriller, third in 'Twisted' trilogy) June 2018, Black Opal Books

The Waffle and the Pancake, (children's picture storybook), September 2018, Bayeux Arts

The Rainbow Vintner, (thriller) February 2019, Black Opal Books

The Fencers, (memoir) March 2019, Deux Voiliers Publishing

Extinction, (poetry collection) April 2019, P.R.A. Publishing

Extinction Rebellion, (poetry collection) July 2020, Cyberwit

Arctic Meltdown, 2nd Updated Edition, (thriller), August 28, 2021, Black Opal Books

The Mind Spins, (short story collection), November 2021, P.R.A. Publishing

The Abyss, (poetry collection), September 2022, P.R.A. Publishing

Arctic Inferno, (thriller), August 5, 2023, Black Opal Books

Geza's website: https://www.gezatatrallyay.com

Contents

Extinction

I can picture the mighty mastodon,
the towering, ivoried, hairy beast
that ruled and roamed this primeval earth

the fierce dinosaurs of the Jurassic,
those huge cold-blooded reptilian beasts
battling each other for primacy

through the microscope of my failing mind
in the imagined black hole of creation
I see tiny single-celled organisms,
the chemical precursors to all life

I ask: when humankind is no longer,
who or what will conceive this strange being
that destroyed earth and all life including
itself as if it had been preordained

Spring wakes up one morning

Spring wakes up one morning
and the world is renewed:
the sun smiles on us as
winter's snow and ice melt,
and earth molts its white coat,
a snake shedding its skin,
trees dress in bright colors
for the summer season,
creeks gush with melt water
and nourishing rains pour,
turning brown grass verdant,
pink and yellow buds appear
and blossom into leaves
or multi-hued flowers,
fiddleheads poke their pates
above the dark topsoil,
unseen peepers chirrup
in transient vernal pools
where ducks land to find food,
robins nest in the eaves
and lay their blue-green eggs—
spring wakes up one morning
and the world is renewed.

Our lilacs are blooming

Our lilacs are blooming,
lavender, pink and white:
their heady fragrance,
sweet, intoxicating,
bewitches my nostrils.
Swallowtail butterflies
flutter from leaf to leaf,
yellow, orange and black,
adding color to the
sensual ecstasy;
a hummingbird hovers
pecking at each flower
to suck up the nectar,
bumblebees, too, buzz
as they flit in and out
competing for their share,
nature's magnificence,
there, alive in one bush!

Will I still be alive?

I am the sinewy buck
that stalks through the forest

I am the vicious wolf
that bares its incisors

I am the wide-winged eagle
that soars above the land

I am the hummingbird
that buzzes the bee balm

I am the sockeye salmon
that saults up waterfalls

I am the princess frog
that jumps in the water

I am the cicada
that plays the night fiddle

I am the mosquito
that bites you and your friend

I am the vile virus
that causes you to die

I am the foul maggot
that eats carrion flesh

will I still be alive
after your killing kind?

A deathly silence reigns out there

A deathly silence reigns out there:
birds do not sing their morning song,
eventide, crickets do not chirp,
there are no frogs left to ribbit,
no dog to bark across the road,
skeleton trees do not sport leaves
to whisk the whisper of the wind,
the heat and drought have killed all life,
corpses litter the land, ours too—
a deathly silence reigns out there.

What color was coral

What color was coral,
now all bleached white?

Multihued it was, once,
before the oceans warmed
and turned more acidic
from all that CO2
we spew into the air,
expelling the algae
living in its polyps
in symbiotic love.

The algae turn toxic,
the coral reefs whither,
nature is diminished,
and beauty is destroyed.

We have done it again.

Mosquito

A wanton mosquito landed
on the bare skin of my forearm,
attacked my feeling flesh with glee,

in a drunken stupor it gorged
through its proboscis on my blood

I swatted the little bugger
with lightening fury and hate,
and squashed it to oblivion,

unmindful of the perfection
of a timeless, evolved being

Over the long torrid summer
my mosquito's countless mates wreak
their revenge on humanity

Haiku: an army of ants

An army of ants
cleans my countertop of crumbs.
Why would I crush them?

Haiku: stardust from heaven

Lighting my way home,
fireflies float among the trees—
stardust from heaven

The chiding cricket

I was dozing spread-eagled on the grass,
when a cricket catapulted onto my crotch,
wiggled its antenna and chided me,
admonishing me for mankind's folly—

yes, the brazen creature took me to task
for our uncaring, polluting lifestyle,
our devastation of its habitat.

I had nothing to say in our defense.

The Dragonfly

I found a dragonfly lazing on our screen door:
a Great Blue Skimmer spreading its filigree wings,
flaunting its dazzling long lapis abdomen
soaking up the warming rays of the noonday sun
oblivious to its Jurassic ancestry

I wonder: will my friend's descendants still be here
one hundred and fifty million years from now,
as we disrupt the equilibrium of earth,
insect outliving cocky Homo sapiens,
the destructive devil of the Anthropocene

A cockroach winked at me ...

A cockroach winked at me from the closet corner,
brazenly taunting the prejudiced human me:

As the beast darted under the soiled laundry pile,
wild with frenzy, I lifted high a much-scuffed shoe
wanting to crush that pestilent cocky creature—

I threw aside the mountain of grubby garments,
and, like Khrushchev banging his desk at the UN,
in the twilight depths of my disordered wardrobe,
blindly bashed away at visions of the beetle

But the insect escaped, scuttling under the boards,
crusty carapace and gangly legs still intact,
to sneak back and goad my ire yet another day

Pollination

A bumblebee buzzes by the bee balm
seeking the blossoms' sweet nectar to suck
with its protracted straw-like proboscis—

inadvertently, it picks up pollen,
brushes it into its corbicula,
packing the fine dust and the propolis
with the pollen press on its hind legs

when the bee alights on the next flower
some of the golden powder brushes off
on the fertile pistil's sticky stigma,
completing magical pollination

next summer's sun will bring forth new blossoms
and bumblebees will pollinate yet again—
unless ... unless, our polluting poisons
devastate their dwindling population.

My poems grow like a tree

My poems grow like a tree,
ideas germinate
in the mind's fertile soil:
tonal words with meaning
emerge, and like fresh shoots,
sprout into rhythmic lines.

New thoughts, new directions
spread their roots, their tendrils,
lo, a metaphor forms—
a freshly budding bough—
and an image blossoms
like a fragrant flower.

Alliterations buzz
like summer bumblebees
in my ecstatic ear—
a perfected picture
with transcendent music,
painted with few words.

The spider's web

A spider spins a spool of spit,
that ever so fine filament,
into a tough, filigree web—
a death trap for wayfaring flies
and other flying bugs and beasts
that it will munch on with delight.

Only the arachnid can scoot
with its long legs along those threads
to get at its perishing prey.

Do not destroy its perfect mesh,
this delicate but sturdy snare
that both destroys and sustains life.

Daddy long legs

a daddy long legs was scrambling on the screen door,
seeming of fragile construction, easy to crush,
daresay, a delicate creature, with eight splayed limbs,
a puff of wind might blow this skull spider away—

but these arachnids are a wonder of nature,
surviving, unchanged for three hundred million years—
better endowed than we, with three pairs of peepers,
they vibrate rapidly to confound predators
and throw their silken web on their mosquito prey

these spiders could teach us peaceful coexistence,
how we might stave off extinction of our species
even as we ravage the world that nurtures us

Fragments of a Moonlit Evening

A misty, translucent peace
drops onto this darkening world
where the sky is washed-out grey,
the land, a sleeping silhouette…

Myriads of crickets chirp,
frightened, aimless in the black night;
now and again some toad croaks—
they all decay, unheard, unsung…

Only the moon, so distant,
asserts itself, illuminates
that unfathomable fog
between my soul and nothingness…

An earthworm

An earthworm pokes its pate
(or might it be its tail?)
up from the soggy lawn

all squiggly and wiggly
it squeezes through the hole
from darkness to the light

and then back down again
the slimy worm burrows
churning through the topsoil

drawing its nourishment
but also nurturing
and aerating the loam

a hermaphroditic
invertebrate creature
so different from man

the creepy night crawler
is beneficial
whereas man just destroys

For a Squashed Land Crab

In the twilight trauma
of the beach at Ixtapa
a land crab sallied forth
from its dungeon in the sand:

he caught my eye in his,
he fathomed me¯
and I think I him:

I willed him life,
life to life,
and he it
back to me¯

but in that marvelous moment
of trans-special spiritflow,
a hulking stud
should trod upon
my comrade crab:

so now the crab is only was,
and my spirit, my eyes, lie limp
bleeding in the sandpapersand.

Crayfish in the Pond

Crayfish have invaded our pond:
those ugly arthropods laid siege
and conquered the massive stone steps
painstakingly laid by the Wards
to ease our way to the water

those yabbies now guard the ramparts
big ones like lobsters, little ones—
more than thirty scamper about
on the underwater platform
copulating to multiply
locking claws in brutal battle

when I hesitatingly step
in the water below the falls
the braver ones tickle my toes
testing the intruding giant

my grandson watches in horror
but I tell him with a chuckle
these little crawdads are harmless
they have survived on mother earth
for fifty plus million years
since the earliest Eocene

without doubt they will outlive us
and the destruction we have brought
on our planet's environment—

climate change, the melting glaciers,
all the wildfires, tempests and floods

they will just go and hibernate,
hide under the rock in the tarn
to reemerge when the sun smiles
on our wasted world once again

Swirls of plastic swim in the seas

Swirls of plastic swim in the seas
deathly fodder for fish, seabirds,
turtles, even dolphins and whales
and ultimately ourselves.

We throw out our used plastic bags
but then end up ingesting them
killing many living beings
unwittingly along the way.

Our profligate stupidity
will result in our extinction.

The Trout

A lone trout inhabits our pond,
curious about the crayfish,
the rotting leaves by the stone steps.

I approach: a flick of the tail
and it plunges effortlessly
into the unfathomable
depths of the watery black hole.

Back in the house, as I listen
to Franz Schubert's sublime quintet,
I wonder: did the fish arrive
by divine magic, as some believe,
the wave of a wand, a god's hand,
the virgin birth of creation,

or drop, a stray fertilized egg
from the palmate of a mallard,
the sheer necessity of chance,
the mere chance of necessity.

The next year my trout is not there.

Haiku: the pond beckons me

the pond beckons me:
crayfish nibble on my toes
my friends, the frogs, croak

Haiku: Angry Clouds

Angry clouds tango
to the music of the frogs,
those thundering gods

The ring-necked snake

Down by our pond I lifted a flat rock:
a squirming, slithering snake startled me,
bedecked in its scaly, grey-black armor,
bright orange neck ring and underbelly—
the serpent's forked tongue darted in and out,
as if wanting to say "This is my space!"

Frightened, at first, I recoiled, then stood back
and admired my reptile friend's perfection
as it slid in silence into a hole,
escaping the human intruder me—

Just for a brief moment, I wondered at
our rather predictable responses,
both my human and the reptilian—
survival, programmed by evolution.

The snake

a scary, scaly snake
slithers across the path,
silent but sensual:

an undulating wave
of ancient foreboding
bringing pause to my steps

but then I check my fear,
revel in the serpent,
evolution's sublime
sample of perfection

Frogs in the Pond

in the late spring gelatinous frogspawn
floats in the pond: undulating streamers
of eggs extruded by the female frog

Marcia my wife attacks them with a rake
pulling them out to dry in the hot sun
against my son's and my loud objections

but she gives up: the task is too daunting
and she will not defeat evolution,
many escape and stay to the next stage

a few weeks go by and in the water
myriads of tadpoles swim and frolic
among the one or two occasional humans

the next time we come there is breaking news:
a royal family of handsome frogs
inhabit the rocks and mud by the pond
hunting flies, mosquitoes and other vermin

metamorphosis has transpired: herbivore
has become carnivore, prey is now predator

I skim the surface swimming lazily
and see four pairs of frog eyes watching me
carefully from under their rocky ledge,
gold dusted eyebrows crowning emerald
green bodies: king, queen, prince and princess frog

Studies in Dislocation

I

A bullfrog ribbits
from the lily pond
waking my senses
from inside silence
to outside thunder.

II

A ghost train whistles
an ominous screech
and derails my brain
from its peaceful track.

III

A telephone rings
and rings in my dream
till I jolt upright:
I rub sleepy eyes
saunter to the phone
and forget the dream.

The traumatized turtle

I came upon a traumatized turtle
playing dead in the middle of the road—
head, legs, tail retracted under her shell,
motionless, all defenses mobilized,
frozen there with fear, in mortal danger
of being crushed to splinters, flesh and blood
by the spinning wheel of a passing truck

I did not know her direction, her goal
but gingerly picked up the armored belle
and placed her on the pond-side of the lane,
wishing that my friend would put the trial
of the traffic, of meeting a human,
all behind her and lay some eggs again.

Seaward blows the wind...

Seaward blows the wind
toward dark and cold
where there are no stars:

Ghostly waves awake
and die shivering
out there in the night.

The somber sky weeps
with tragic fury
or mocking laughter.

A lonely seagull
screeches in the gale:
the vulture of hope.

Frantic in the dusk,
my mind is flooded
with aching questions
that bear no answers.

Evening: Heron and Pond

dusk silence

a gray heron
skates gracefully
over the pond
    a blade slicing
    the oil fleck
    shimmering through
    tarry forest greens

a violent flutter
of pterodactyl wings
the bird evolves
into a receding
silhouette against
a polyphonic sky
    vermilion
    and indigo
    aquamarine
    and burnt orange

A rafter of wild turkeys ...

A rafter of wild turkeys frolics in the field:
some toms and hens, young jakes and jennies, a few poults,
the birds strut and prance, then go pecking and poking,

they halt for a moment at the side of the road
and in a burst, vault out onto the macadam,
high-tailing it across the dangerous divide—

relief! they have made it, even the smallest chick—

bravo, say I, rooting for the rafter to live:

but ... in my gut, I, the glutton, think to myself:
would that meaty hen not have made a tasty meal?

The hummingbird

Azure and jade and gold
a hummingbird flutters
dancing to the music
sung by evolution

its slender beak seeking
the nectar of flowers
helping to spread pollen
for next summer's rebirth

its wings' rapid flapping
allowing it to float
from flower to flower
fertilizing who's next

nature, life will go on
unless our consumptive
depravity destroys
this garden of Eden

The dead phoebe

I found a phoebe on the porch—
she lay there, dead, I know not why.

I wondered: did she have children,
how many eggs has she hatched,
how many have flown from her nest,
will the bird be missed by anyone
but me, who heard her call her name,
fee-bee, fee-bee, when I approached?

Now that my phoebe is no more,
will anyone miss me when I die?

The Canada geese have landed

The Canada geese have landed
and festooned our fields with feces:
my wife attacks them with a broom,
an otherworldly scream drowns out
the cackling of the flying rats—
her shriek, like that of a banshee,
scares the unwanted fowl away.
They take off, skimming the water,
and still honking, flapping their wings,
they disappear into the sky,
as Marcia, pleased with herself,
struts slowly back up from the pond.

The birds are gone, for now, at least.

But the next year, the beasts are back,
and the game of defecating,
chasing, screeching, wing fluttering,
escaping is played out once more.

And the next year, and the next year,
the spectacle unfolds yet again:
nature's drama, while it still can.

Haiku: no stars

No stars, cloudy night,
a loon's tremolo portends,
calamity looms

Haiku: glide across the sky

Glide across the sky,
glibly, behind the crest of
a pterodactyl …

The Kingfisher

A kingfisher perches atop
a rocking chair down by the pond,
he sits there, regally attired
in his blue-grey and white armor,
surveying his Vermont empire.

On the chair and the ground below,
skeletal remains of crayfish
the king consumed are strewn around
as he holds forth up on his throne,
with the occasional flutter
of wings to pluck yet another
crustacean from the dark waters.

Torrential rain falls, thunderstorms,
yet the royal beast does not leave
his post: drenched but composed, he stays
to thrill us yet another day.

A field mouse shares our house ...

A field mouse shares our house
when we are in Vermont,
retiring discretely
to its hole in the wall,
to escape my wife's wrath.

All it wants is a crumb,
or better still, leftovers,
a warm nook in the cold,
a corner to nest in,
to give birth to its brood.

I ask my better half,
why not let the beast be?
Why set out a mousetrap,
the bloody guillotine,
to execute our friend?

Alarum

the plangent wail of a Siren shrieking
grates above the rubble of imminent
destruction:

                    our imperfect ears refuse
to admit the Stentor's admonition

'though all around,
                              rat and 'roach
                                            flee
                                                      panic-
stricken,
    from this concrete Sodom,
                                            this Hell,

while we,
                    the cognoscenti,
                                            lovingly

unite, to raise a tower of Babel
(building Chaos with our bombs and missiles)

Toward a heaven that we think we know

Squirrel

That rustling sound from under the brown
blanket that covers our black earth—

Is it a squirrel scurrying
to find that last morsel before
cold and white bleach the living world?

The Hare

Albrecht Dürer's perfect "Young Hare"
has lived more than five hundred years,
admired in royal collections,
and now in the Albertina,
it survives with our loving care.

But hares evolved on earth more than
fifty million years ago:
will Dürer's depiction outlast
them and us as we drive most life
to unrepentant extinction?

What irony if this painting
outlives the creature it depicts
with no one left to admire it!

The seals were barking ...

The seals were barking in the night
down by the Embarcadero,
happy the tourists were not there
and they had the world to themselves

but morning comes again, too soon
and brings the swarming multitudes
with all their filth and pollution
for yet another dreary day

The Dead Coyote

(hiking in the desert)

Packing the Pushawalla trail,
across the path, in the hot sun,
we stumbled on the dead coyote:
a shot had ripped through its stomach,
then some vermin gutted the beast,
now rotting, though fur still fluffy,
redolent of fading splendor,
this once warm, sentient being
hunts the forests and fields no more

what callous thug killed it and why?

The Black Rhinoceros

(after a safari at Lewa Downs, Kenya)

The black rhinoceros is a bizarre old beast,
a crash of them on the move is a fearful sight:
loose folds of leathery skin, wrinkled and dirt-caked
sheathe that prodigious, sagging, brawny old physique
barely held off the ground by those stocky pillars;
the ungulate's keen schnozzle smells you from afar,
the floppy ears perk up to catch the faintest sound,
those half-blind peepers vainly strain to seek you out—
two slender, tapered sabers protrude from the snout,
horns worth more than gold to poachers from East Asia
who butcher these splendid endangered animals
and leave their carcasses to rot in the hot sun.
Like other magnificent species on this earth,
we have driven this creature close to extinction.

The Bear

Trekking the Royalton Turnpike,
while squashing a pesky deer fly,
I catch sight of a big black bear
crossing the road fifty yards up—
I stop in my tracks, dare not move …

A penetrating look, a wink—
ursus licks its lips, bares its teeth
at the cowering spectator
and with a wag of its buttocks,
disappears into the forest.

Polar Bears

Climate change warms the atmosphere:
the Arctic polar ice cap melts
and vainly struggles to re-form—
polar bears visit villages
along the Siberian coast;
famished, they forage for food scraps,
dig up corpses of walruses,
they cannot go out on the ice
to hunt for ringed seals and sea hares—
they are wasted, their babies die,
their habitat destroyed by man—
how long before they go extinct?

In early December 2019, about 60 polar bears were reported to have descended on the village of Ryrkaypiy in Russia's remote Chukotka region in search of food, because the sea ice was too thin for them to pursue their usual hunt.

Haiku: a whale kills a man

A whale kills a man:
how many whales have we killed
to harvest blubber?

Dream, choreographed

Background: Bleak
hillock,
leafless trees,
obscure sky:

Foreground: my
black back,
and I
gazing
in terror
toward
the stark mound:

And in between: a white steed,
translucent,
yes, ghost-like,
gallops among dead trees
toward the horizon.

Aftermath: I wake,
the dream
vanishes,
and then
even
its memory dies.

Elusive anthropoid ...

Even though we destroy
your luscious habitat,

brother orangutan,
wise man of the jungle,
elusive anthropoid,

you gaze at me with peace
and woe and wonder,
sitting there regally
up on your tree-top perch
in the nest you crafted
so skillfully last night—

your flaming orange hair
glistens in the sunlight
before you disappear
in the high canopy
of greens and browns and blues ...

how many more sightings,

brother orangutan,
wise man of the jungle,
elusive anthropoid,

before you are extinct,
and then how much longer
until mankind follows?

We are the masked great ape ...

Our faces are covered:
we are the masked great ape,
now cowering in fear
of some nano-virus.

This pandemic panic
destroys our livelihoods,
strains our relationships,
reshapes society.

But better still alive,
still breathing and feeling,
than buried underground
in some improvised grave.

We are the masked great ape,
no longer absolute
ruler of this jungle,
the world we have ruined.

Questions for us

Our fellow species on this earth
are magnificent, eccentric beasts,
creations of evolution
over many millennia.

Why do we not respect them more,
these other wondrous forms of life?

Why do we murder them for food,
or willy-nilly for pleasure,
burn the woods and steppes they live in,
pour chemicals and shit into
the rivers and lakes where they swim?

Why do we poison the water,
so necessary for all life,
pollute the air we and they breathe?

Why are we recklessly driving
us all to shameful extinction?

We find reasons to kill …

Why swat a fly when it flies in your face?
A mosquito that tries to bite your arm?
Why cull a crayfish that swims in your pond?
Why trap a mouse that likes to share your house?
Why shoot a fox that chews up your chickens?
Why slaughter a pig to devour its chops?
Why butcher a bull that skewers your son?
Why murder a neighbor who screws your wife?

We find reasons to kill other beings
To justify our murdering instinct
Instead of existing in peace with them.

Alas, my friend Darwin

To survive, to live on,
at almost any cost
is life's strongest instinct—
it must be genetic,
deep in our DNA
a potent agent of
natural selection.

But Homo sapiens
is changing the climate,
its own environment,
making much of the world
near inhospitable
for many forms of life,
sadly, including us,
as we cannot adapt,
alter our errant ways
fast enough to survive
the berserk destruction
we have unleashed on earth.

Alas, my friend Darwin,
mankind will go the way
of the woolly mammoth.

Haiku: the bat and the pangolin

We abuse nature—
the bat and the pangolin,
their virus kills us

Homo postcoronavirus

We are all premature corpses:
death masks now cover our faces
as we walk around like zombies,
not touching, feeling or hugging
our fellow ghost-like creatures.

We quake with the frigid frisson
of fear that we might just crumble
into viral dust with the next breath.

At night we return to our tombs
of anxiety and terror,
and wake to morbid statistics.

Will there be at least one Adam
and one Eve who survive this plague
to spawn a new kind of being?

One, who will treat this world better,
not destroy its fellow species,
the land, sea and air all around,
a wiser and kinder human,
Homo postcoronavirus.

The world, a wasteland humans shaped

The world, a wasteland humans shaped,
where we, the self-declared apex
of all life wantonly wage war
on our fellow living beings
with our bombs, tanks and cruise missiles

the profligate lifestyle we lead,
where money is all that matters,
and we ignore our climate woes:

wildfires, drought, wild tempests and floods,
rage out of control and destroy
the planet's beauty all around

alas, there is no going back

About the Poet

Born in Budapest, Hungary, Geza Tatrallyay escaped with his family in 1956 during the Revolution, immigrating to Canada the same year. He attended the University of Toronto Schools, where he was School Captain. He graduated from Harvard University with a BA in Human Ecology in 1972 (after taking a break in his studies to work as a host in the Ontario Pavilion at Expo'70 in Osaka, Japan). As a Rhodes Scholar from Ontario, he attended Oxford University, graduating with a BA/MA in Human Sciences in 1974; followed by a MSc in Economics from London School of Economics and Politics in 1975. Geza represented Canada as an epée fencer in the 1976 Olympic Games in Montreal. His professional experience has included stints in government, international organizations, finance and environmental entrepreneurship. Since 2004, he has been semi-retired, managing investments in the clean energy sector and devoting himself to his family and his writing. He is an author and a poet, with sixteen books (six thrillers, five poetry collections, three memoirs, a short story collection and a children's picture story book) published by different authors in the U.S.A., Canada and India. He has also just completed a Vermont-based murder mystery, *The Purple School Bus Murders,* which he hopes to bring out in 2024. Geza's poetry collections are: *Cello's Tears* (2015), *Sighs and Murmurs* (2018), *Extinction* (2019), *Extinction Rebellion* (2020) and *The Abyss: Poems for our World* (2022). His poems, short stories and articles have appeared in journals, magazines and anthologies in Canada and the USA. Geza is a citizen of Canada and Hungary, and a green card holder, currently divides his time between Barnard, Vermont, and San Francisco. He is married to Marcia, and their daughter, Alexandra, lives in San Francisco with husband David, and two sons, Sebastian and Orlando, while their son, Nicholas, lives in Nairobi with his Hungarian wife, Fanni, and his granddaughters, Sophia and Lara.

Website: http://www.gezatatrallyay.com

Acknowledgements

Fragments of a Moonlit Evening, Haiku: fossil shells, Frogs in the Pond, Evening: Heron and Pond, Seaward blows the wind and *Squirrel* were published in my first collection, ***Cello's Tears*** by P.R.A. Publishing in 2015.

For a Squashed Land Crab, Studies in Dislocation, Alarum and *Dream, choreographed* were published in my second collection, ***Sighs and Murmurs***, by P.R.A. Publishing in 2017.

Extinction, Mosquito, The Trout, The Dragonfly, Haiku: an army of ants, Elusive Anthropoid, Crayfish in the Pond, A cockroach winked at me, Haiku: Cretacean Fantasy were published in my third collection, ***Extinction*** by P.R.A. Publishing in 2019.

The Trout also appeared in ***Polar Expressions*** in December 2017; *Extinction* and *The Dragonfly* in ***Grey Borders Magazine*** in August 2018.

Will I still be alive?, Pollination, The chiding cricket, Daddy long legs, An earthworm, The ring-necked snake, The traumatized turtle, The hummingbird, The Canada geese have landed, A rafter of wild turkeys ..., A field mouse shares our house, The Hare, The seals were barking, The Dead Coyote, The Black Rhinoceros, The Bear, Polar Bears, Haiku: glide across the sky, Alas my friend, Darwin and *Haiku: the bat and the pangolin* were published in my fourth collection, ***Extinction Rebellion*** by Cyberwit in 2020.

Pollination also appeared in the 2020 ***PoemTown Anthology*** put out by the town of Randolph VT, and *The Hare*, has been published in Volume LXVI of ***The Mountain Troubadour***, 2020.

The spider's web, A black, ringed snake, The dead phoebe,

Spring wakes up one morning, Our lilacs are blooming, Haiku: the bond beckons me, Haiku: stardust from heaven, Haiku: Angry clouds, Haiku: no stars, My poems grow like a tree, Questions for us, Swirls of plastic swim in the seas, What color was coral, Haiku: a whale kills a man, We find reasons to kill, We are the masked great ape, Alas, my friend Darwin, Haiku: a bat and a pangolin and *Homo postcoronavirus* were all published in my fifth poetry collection, ***The Abyss: Poems for our World*** September 2022 by Deux Voiliers Publishing.

What color was coral and *Homo postcoronavirus* were published in ***Terror House Magazine*** in April 2021.

Homo postcoronavirus was posted in store windows in ***Poem Town***, St. Johnsbury VT during Poetry Month, April 2021 and also included in the ***Vermont History COVID Archive.***

The Kingfisher was published in the 2023 ***PoemCity Anthology*** put out by the town of Montpelier VT.

www.ingramcontent.com/pod-product-compliance
Lightning Source LLC
Chambersburg PA
CBHW031522180726
48282CB00056B/297
9788119654857